FAST
TRACK

TO SUCCESSFUL SELLING

Mastering Selling
in Minutes

Fast-Track to Successful Selling

Mastering Selling in Minutes

Richard Denny

urbanepublications.com

First published in Great Britain in 2015
by Urbane Publications Ltd
Suite 3, Brown Europe House,
33/34 Gleamingwood Drive,
Chatham, Kent ME5 8RZ

Copyright © Richard Denny, 2015

The moral right of Richard Denny to be identified as the author of this work has been asserted in accordance with the Copyright, Designs and Patents Act of 1988.

All rights reserved. No part of this publication may be reproduced, stored in a retrieval system, or transmitted in any form or by any means, electronic, mechanical, photocopying, recording or otherwise, without the prior permission of both the copyright owner and the above publisher of this book.

A CIP catalogue record for this book is available from the British Library.

ISBN 978-1-909273-67-2
EPub 978-1-909273-68-9

Design and Typeset by Chandler Design

Printed in Great Britain by
CPI Group (UK) Ltd,
Croydon, CR0 4YY

urbanepublications.com

The publisher supports the Forest Stewardship Council® (FSC®), the leading international forest-certification organisation. This book is made from acid-free paper from an FSC®-certified provider. FSC is the only forest-certification scheme supported by the leading environmental organisations, including Greenpeace.

TESTIMONIALS

"Richard Denny is the Master of Sales and his books are masterpieces of sales advice."

Bev James, Founder, MD & Head of Training for the Entrepreneurs' Business Academy

"His engaging straight-talking, humorous and highly professional style mirrors his powerful prose."

Professor Colin Turner, author

"From the beginner to the hardened old pro, this is the book that you have to carry if you want to sell."

Geoff Burch, global business guru

"Richard Denny is that rare combination – a sales genius with the ability to translate his profound knowledge into simple steps that you can follow to transform your sales. This book contains the keys to unlocking the financial freedom you deserve. Buy it. Read it. Use it."

Chris Cardell, business adviser

> "Richard Denny is an amazing communicator. Follow Richard Denny's advice and you cannot fail!"
>
> **Rosemary Conley, CBE**

> "I was first introduced to Richard Denny over 10 years ago. In that time his words have inspired many, and the stories have stayed as a precious reminder to help achieve customer excellence and to build long term relationships."
>
> **Diane Martyn, Non-Executive Director, Staffline Group Plc**

> "I just made a £3k sale today by thinking a no is a later yes, thanks to your book. That's a ROI of 300x!"
>
> **Johannes Anderson, web design consultant**

Contents

Introduction	1
1. Can you sell?	5
2. Identify your customers	17
3. Selling in-house	31

Retail outlets; Telephone enquiries; E-mail enquiries; Shows and exhibitions; Internet

4. Selling out-house 47

The telephone call; The letter; E-mail; Voicemail; Some tips on making excellent telephone calls

5. Planning and preparation 63

Prepare yourself for sales meetings; Product knowledge; Read the person; Speak slowly; Time; Goals and targets; Rehearse

6. Sales expertise 75

Sell yourself; Ask the right questions; Listen well; Link features and benefits Sell the results; Identify your unique sales points (USPs); Don't knock the competition; Understand buying emotions; Listen and learn; Names and detail; It's not what you say; Be positive; Self-motivation

7. The classic presentation 97

Stage one – getting yourself accepted; Stage two – getting attention; Stage three - asking the right questions; Stage four - checking; Stage five – the marriage; Stage six – the final check; Stage seven – the close

8. Objections to reassurance 109
Prevention is better than cure; Stage one – ask back; Stage two – agree and outweigh; Stage three – provide the answer

9. Be proud of your price 117
Price-condition; 'What is the discount?'

10. Presenting a proposal 127
How to present a proposal

11. Great tips for sales success! 135

12. Why Richard Denny Equals Sales Success! 139

About the author 145

Introduction

Selling has been universally in demand from the beginning of anthropological time and is often claimed to be one of the two oldest professions. I question whether the current classification of sales people as 'professionals' sits comfortably with other classifications of professional such as lawyers, accountants, doctors, vets and so on. Nevertheless, whether we like it or not, nothing happens anywhere in the world until a sale takes place and the seller brings in the money that everybody can eventually live off.

Digital platforms have dramatically changed dramatically the way most businesses do business, whether it is business to business (B2B) or business to customer (B2C). This has led to a considerable decrease in the number of people employed just to sell, whilst at the same time there has been a massive increase in the number of people with a secondary responsibility to sell, either to bring in new business or to maximise the potential from existing customers or clients.

In the United Kingdom and elsewhere, sales people have been devalued for far too long. Managers have convinced themselves that sales people are difficult to handle, demand new cars, fiddle their expense accounts and are a very expensive commodity. The buying public have rarely appreciated the value of sales people, and can regard them as pushy and insincere, persuading people to buy things that they really do not want. So sales people try not to admit that selling is what they do. They give themselves spurious titles like 'executives', 'consultants' and 'advisers'. Sadly, this reputation has been partly earned, and the mistrust in many cases has been deserved through bad practice.

In the retail sector, the customer frustration has been caused by employers not investing in training their sales assistants. As we all

INTRODUCTION

know, it is a great pleasure and an enjoyable experience to be sold to well. The majority of us like buying, and it is a great joy when the sales person helps to give us a good experience, something which is really not difficult to do.

Probably the best definition of modern sales people is that they are 'solution specialists'. This is a rather glamorous title, but nevertheless it describes the real activity of successful selling, which is problem solving. I don't want to devalue the concept of a sales person being a solution specialist, but we are continually hearing of lofty titles for fairly mundane work. The latest addition for my book of titles is 'underwater hand technician' – which is apparently someone who washes dishes.

The purpose of this book is to provide a common-sense, businesslike approach to selling and winning business that will give the reader the confidence and the skills to sell successfully and professionally.

So let's get started.

1

Can you sell?

Can you sell or, more importantly, do you want to sell? Very few people, when they were at school or university, chose selling as their future career. My research has shown that most sales people got the job by opportunity or necessity. In the last few years there has been a massive change of emphasis, with non-sales people actively taking ownership of winning new clients and developing those relationships into new business opportunities. As a result people who previously would never, not even in their wildest imaginations, have thought that part of their profession would be selling, are in fact doing just that.

Through necessity and to keep themselves employed, people have been forced into learning the skills of selling. So can you sell? Of course you can, but only if you really want to. It is probably worth noting, as a motivation and a stimulus, that as you become successful at winning new business you will also increase your income, and for most people this is a good enough reason.

A common belief is that a good sales person can sell anything. We have all heard the expression 'He or she could sell fridges to Eskimos.' I take issue with the statement that good sales people can sell anything. They can't. Good and successful sales people can sell only what they believe in. It is therefore worth establishing at the outset what good sales people actually do. Very simply it is that, given the chance of meeting a prospective customer, they will complete the transaction and close the sale. Equally they must create an environment and experience that will make the customer come and buy again.

Once a sales person has built that trust and relationship, the customer will recommend the sales person or the company to friends, family and connections. This is what professional selling can achieve. This is what you can do comparatively easily.

Therefore it is imperative that you have belief in your product or service. You must convince yourself of the value and the results that your product or service will achieve for your customers. Now it is essential at this stage to mention price, though this will be covered in more detail in Chapter 9. There will be many occasions when your product or service will not be the cheapest, but this must not impede your belief in it. What matters here is that your product or service delivers what you state it will, what is claimed or what the customer is looking for. If it does that, the price is of less importance.

It is often stated that we were all born with the ability to sell, as exemplified by the persuasive skills of children (as well as by some questionable tactics that cannot be used in business). Nevertheless, the skills and tactics achieve the desired result for children. Then young people gradually become educated, and there is one word that creates such an inhibitor in fertile minds that it not only blocks the enthusiasm to sell but also prevents young people from achieving so much more. That one word is **'No'**.

This word 'No' is construed in the human brain as a word of rejection, which in most cases it certainly is not. The fear that someone will say 'No' to us not only prevents us from getting involved in selling but also holds us back from so many of life's opportunities.

This is probably the most important principle that every aspiring sales person should embrace. Disregard this chapter at your peril. A 'No' is only ever a 'No, not today'. When anyone ever says 'No' to you, it is only 'No' at that moment in time. You have almost certainly bought something or done something in the last six months that previously you said 'No' to. Why? Because circumstances will have changed, and this is exactly the same for your potential customers. As your sales career develops you will find that your and your company's biggest revenue stream will come from your existing customers. Your second biggest revenue stream will come from what you now call your 'No, not todays'.

Your third biggest business stream will come from new customers.

When you meet a prospective customer there are two possible outcomes. You will get some business, make a sale or have an order, or you will get a 'No, thank you', which if you handle it well is only a 'No, not today'. Now I am not saying that you should be a pushy individual. Ninety-seven per cent of people don't like pushy people, and pushy sales people do exactly that - push prospective customers away. The reverse principle is so much more effective, and that is to be a 'pully' person. Draw your prospective customers to you.

When you get a 'No' this is what you can do:

> *'Thank you. Can we keep the door open? I would like to ring you in three or four months' time, as your circumstances may change and we may have something else that we can offer you.'*

You will almost certainly get a 'Yes', and I recommend that you then say:

> *'Fine, I will give you a call again in three to four months.'*

Take out your diary and (assuming your meeting was on 15 May) say:

> *'OK, I'll give you a call again round about the 15th of September. Is that OK? In the meantime, may I keep you informed by e-mail or post of our new products or services?'*

You will invariably get another 'Yes'.

Now it is very important to get the balance right here and to maintain contact with a bit of news not more than monthly. It must be only items that are genuinely of interest to that prospective customer. Be realistic. There are of course occasions when there is no chance because there is no synergy between your product or service and your customer.

When it is time to arrange the new appointment you can commence your telephone conversation with:

'Mr/Ms...? When I was with you in May we agreed that I would call you in September to arrange a short meeting to explain our latest products or services. I don't know how your diary is fixed, but may I suggest...?'

Let's revert to the theme of this chapter. Can you sell? You can, once you have developed a mindset that selling is not about making people buy something that they don't want but about helping prospective customers to make up their own minds. It is your responsibility to provide accurate information so that customers are in the best possible position to do just that.

From now on, whenever you have the opportunity to meet or talk to a prospective customer, you are either going to get a sale or you will be getting a 'No, not today'. You cannot fail. With this in mind your subconscious brain will remove the biggest impediment to selling, which is the fear of failure or rejection. You will be amazed at how much business over the years will come from your 'No, not today' contacts.

The emphasis of modern selling is to develop what is known as relationship and consultative selling. Both of those adjectives will be explained in more detail in the following chapters. Suffice to say at this stage that it is much easier to win new business from a person who you have developed a relationship with rather than a complete stranger.

We have all heard sales people brag that they do business with X, Y and Z company. I have tried over the years to sell to companies, to the private sector and the public sector, to government bodies and institutions, to homes and flats, and I have never achieved a sale. I have only ever made a sale to another person. So your marketplace is no different from mine. Selling is about relationships, trust and earning respect.

In building relationships you must become a good ambassador of your product or your company, and to do this you will need six vital ingredients:

1. business knowledge

2. industry knowledge

3. company knowledge

4. product knowledge

5. sales skills

6. attitude

Business knowledge

The sales person should be able to converse with clients or customers on all aspects of the business climate and marketing trends. This information is of course gleaned from the world's press and media.

Industry knowledge

To be effective, sellers must be familiar with their industry and with their competitors' products, prices and positioning. They should be aware of people and personalities within their industry and trade bodies. They must be aware of their competitors' main selling points and new product releases. This information is readily available in the trade press.

Company knowledge

Sales people should be aware of company policy and people. They should be informed about their company's marketing and advertising and should know the right departments and people to go to for advice and support.

Product knowledge

Now this is really crucial in today's marketplace. Sales people must be able to give excellent and accurate information on their product portfolio. They must be credible, and their job is to impart to prospective customers answers to questions and concerns.

Sales skills

It is essential to have the sales skills of this millennium and not the last. These will need continuing refreshment.

Attitude

This is of course the ultimate characteristic that distinguishes the superstars from the also-rans. A positive and enthusiastic attitude will become the major ingredient not only in developing relationships but also in winning a great deal of new business and earning your clients' trust, which will lead to recommendations and referrals. A positive attitude is the single most desired attribute of a successful sales person.

So, once again, can you sell? Yes, of course you can if you really want to and are willing to spend a little time developing the skills.

Key Questions

- Will being good at selling advance my career?
- Is a 'No' an opportunity?
- Do I keep a 'No, not today' list?
- Do I keep in regular contact with 'No, not todays'?
- Am I keeping up to date with current affairs?
- Do I read my trade press?
- Am I a good ambassador for my company?

2

Identify your customers

Who do you want to sell to? Or, more importantly, who is most likely to want to purchase your products or use your services? Not identifying the customers is probably one of the major errors that sales people make. This oversight is even more common with people who set up their own businesses. People can get into business with an enthusiasm and belief in their product or service and then in many cases waste a great deal of money in advertising and targeting too broad a customer base. This is the shotgun approach as opposed to the rifle approach, which is much more targeted.

You must draw up a very clear customer profile. This of course varies according to your product or service. If you are in B2B you must define exactly the businesses that would most benefit from your product or service. If you are in B2C, again clearly define the customer who would most benefit from your product or service. The profile could include age, sex, socioeconomic standing and similar purchases that the customer is currently making.

The second stage, if you are in B2B, is to draw up a list of potential customers within a five-mile radius. These can be readily sourced from directories, from local papers and by being observant when driving around. I stress the importance of this, as so much time can be wasted in travelling. It is incredibly effective to build a customer base locally rather than nationally. B2B selling normally requires the sales person to go to customer's premises, whereas B2C is normally the reverse.

I think that it is worth clarifying that the advice in this book is not intended for internet marketing, which immediately highlights a difference. People often confuse selling and marketing. For many people marketing sounds more acceptable than selling. Let me attempt to distinguish these two very important activities.

Marketing encompasses advertising, branding, PR, sales brochures, labelling and packaging – all of which are intended to create potential customer interest, but then selling takes over. Selling involves person-to-person communication, either on the phone or face to face. Now I do accept that some selling takes place on the internet, which is of course based on words and pictures. With regard to the internet, which is getting more and more sophisticated, not only does it require that you have an excellent website that within three seconds of customers clicking on it must retain their interest, but it must also be very easy for customers to find what they are looking for. The real sophistication comes in the marketing of the website and search engine optimisation (SEO), so that the site comes in high on the list selected by the search engines. The whole process of winning business this way carries high risk, because the seller is dependent on customers finding the website. It also can be dangerous because this is a passive activity where the future is dependent on customers, and you could easily go broke waiting for the phone to ring or the order to arrive by e-mail.

Proactive marketing and selling are entirely in your control. You will decide how many people you will approach, and by increasing your activity here you will undoubtedly increase your sales. Selling after all is really a numbers game. The more people you talk to, the more likely you are to win business.

In our executive recruitment division, which is probably in one of the most competitive industries, where advertising your services is a complete waste of money, winning new clients is totally dependent on the number of outgoing approaches that are made to prospective customers. It is a very simple formula – the more contacts that our sales people make, the more successful they will be.

I personally recommend that every business should be operating both proactively and passively. Of course, it is essential to have a website, and for any readers who want further advice on this, contact us at success@denny.co.uk

I stated above that, for B2B selling, it is wise to start by building a list of potential customers within a five-mile radius. This may not be pertinent in some instances, and that radius may have to be 10 or even 20 miles, but the principle is important.

I have advised numerous franchise companies over the years, and in most cases a franchisee buys a given territory. This can be based on postcodes, counties or population. Nevertheless, when a new franchisee starts business, they should concentrate on distributing their marketing literature in most cases within a one-mile radius of their base and then gradually move out. It is often fascinating to see how much potential business there can be within a one-mile radius, and it is so much more cost-effective, as vans with company logos that are continually seen can generate new enquiries. We all know that success in advertising comes from the repetition, not just the one sighting.

B2B requires a much more detailed and planned approach. Every sales person, unless starting with a virgin product or virgin territory, will no doubt have some existing customers. It therefore makes sense to compile as much data as possible.

Once you have identified the target companies, the next stage is to compile the detail in order to make the right contacts. Remember, we don't sell to companies; we sell to people. This leads to another frustrating yet common mistake made by sales people, and that is having a meeting with the wrong person, who invariably is not the decision maker. So, having compiled the list of customers, you now need to get the right contacts. You must decide the job title of the person most likely to be the decision maker, with the biggest interest in your product or service. The information you need is:

- company name
- contact
- job title
- telephone number
- e-mail
- other contacts (personal assistant, secretary, etc)

It will be necessary for you to get up-to-date and accurate details, which can very rarely be acquired through directories, as there is constant migration of people from company to company. You will almost certainly have the company name and telephone number. Here are two examples of the telephone call that you can make to obtain information.

Example one

Dial the company number. When the receptionist answers, use these words and only these words:

> ***Receptionist:*** *Joe Bloggs Engineering.*
>
> ***You:*** *Can you help me, please?*
>
> ***Receptionist:*** *I will if I can.*
>
> ***You:*** *I have been asked to send a letter to the person responsible for… and I don't have that person's name.*
>
> *The receptionist will respond with the name.*
>
> ***You:*** *Thank you. What is the person's first name?*
>
> *The receptionist will give you the name.*
>
> ***You:*** *So Mr/Ms X is responsible for…?*

The most important part of the above example is the words 'Can you help me, please?' Please don't vary this, and when you say the words your voice must drop down at the end of the sentence.

Example two

You: *Is that X Company?*

Receptionist: *Yes (or company name)*

You: *I'm just addressing an envelope – is your post-code GL21 4FW?*

Receptionist: *Yes (or the postcode will be corrected).*

You: *So that's 7 Queensmead Trading Estate, Shrimpton-on-Sea?*

Receptionist: *Yes (or the correct address will follow).*

You: *I am sending an invitation for… To whom do I address the invitation?*

Receptionist: *Mr/Ms X.*

You: *What is his/her position in the company/firm/practice?*

> ***Receptionist:*** *Managing director/sales director/partner.*

In my group of companies every fee earner has a list of 50 potential customers that we want to win, and that is a good target for all sales people to set for themselves. These can be called your key prospects. The time spent on preparing this detail will reap untold rewards.

As a sales person you have assets and resources available to you. Your most valuable asset is of course your brain, and it is valuable to you if it is thinking positively, expecting to win, expecting to succeed and looking forward to the future. If you are in a negative frame of mind, full of self-doubt, living in the past or lacking confidence, this requires some serious attention. May I recommend my book ***Succeed for Yourself***, which has made a major contribution to thousands of people's lives in fulfilment, happiness and success. But I would say that, wouldn't I? However, this is what my postbag tells me.

Now your major resource is a kind of bank account, one that we all have in common.

This bank account has some peculiarities. You can never get a statement. You can never make a deposit. All you can do is withdraw from it. This is of course your bank account of time. With this bank account you have no manager with whom you can discuss the most effective use of its assets. And you never know how much you have left in it. So time is your most valuable resource.

There is such a very big difference between activity and achievement. A person can be very busy all day long without actually achieving very much. This person can be mentally and physically exhausted at the end of a day and will often voice the expression 'I don't know where the time has gone but I haven't stopped all day.' Such individuals have not set themselves clearly defined goals or tasks, and they often suffer from the human frailty of procrastination. They put off or forget things they should be doing or should have done. In order for your brain to function really well, it needs to know that it is progressing. We are all more motivated when we see ourselves achieving, progressing and on top of what we know in our heart of hearts we should be doing.

It is impossible to manage time. Whether we like it or not, we cannot get more than 24 hours in a day and 60 minutes in an hour. What we are all in control of is what we do in those minutes and hours. I do not know of any person who achieves success (and let me clarify immediately that success should not be judged in monetary terms) who does not operate a time management system.

With regard to the sales person, in the most simplistic form the day can be divided as follows:

TWT: This stands for 'total working time'. This is the hours of the day allocated for work. This may be nine to five or whatever.

CCT: This stands for 'customer contact time'. This is the time actually spent in contact with customers and potential customers.

I challenge you right now to write in the box below what percentage of your TWT is currently spent on CCT.

If you are average, CCT will be approximately 14 per cent. So where is the rest of your time spent? Again, if you are average, it will be spent on driving, coffee breaks, parking, preparing for meetings, internal meetings and conversation, talking internally, preparing reports for internal use, and of course surfing the internet. Now set yourself a realistic goal.

Now let me warn you. If you increase your CCT, you will absolutely and without question increase your sales and hopefully your income.

The simplest time management system, and generally the simplest is the most effective, is the 'to do' list, which most of us are aware of. Sadly, the concept of a daily 'to do' list is incorrectly used. If you seriously want to create greater fulfilment in your life, be less pressurised and achieve more, follow exactly this advice:

1. Always prepare your 'to do' list as soon as you have finished work for the day. It is your last business task. Do not do what most people do and compile your list as the first activity of the new day.

2. Having compiled the complete list of jobs or tasks to do the following day, number that list in order of importance. In most cases you will find that the most important is nearly always the most unpleasant. It does not matter how many tasks you have on your list.

3. The following day when you decide to start work, and this often differs from the time you go into work, start at number one and work on it until it is complete and then tackle number two until it is complete and so on through the list. If you follow the above system and you only complete four of a list of 20, there is no known other way of getting more done in a day. The four that you have completed were the most important. This in itself is highly motivational for your brain.

One further bit of advice for sales people is to prioritise your tasks. Your most important priority is any activity that will generate revenue, ie dealing with a customer complaint or making six proactive calls or preparing a quotation or maybe following up on a previous call.

Finally, when utilising this most wonderful bank account that we all have, be conscious of not allowing other people to waste your time. They are stealing from your bank account, and that equally applies to you. Are you wasting your own time?

Key Questions

- Do I have a website?
- Is it managed?
- Have I a 50-prospects list?
- Am I currently adding to the list?
- Have I set a goal to increase my CCT?
- Do I compile a 'to do' list prior to switching off?
- Do I always do the worst job first?

Selling in-house

Retail outlets; Telephone enquiries; E-mail enquiries; Shows and exhibitions; Internet

The chapter title is of course not literal. It is about the situation when the customer comes to you as opposed to you, the seller, going to the customer, which will be covered in the following chapter. Selling of this nature is referred to as business to customer (B2C).

The five key areas for in-house selling are:

1. retail outlets

2. telephone enquiries

3. e-mail enquiries

4. shows and exhibitions

5. internet

Each one of the above naturally requires a different process of handling customers effectively.

Retail outlets

This covers the vast majority of all consumer purchasing and goes from food shopping through to the motor trade, clothes shopping and garden centres. It is of course impossible in this book to cover every trade, and anyhow that is not the purpose of this sales guide. As I have already stated, it is about selling to people in every situation.

Even though you may be reading this book to develop your skills to become a successful sales person, you are also a customer. It is therefore essential, if you are to succeed as a preferred sales person (in other words, customers want to talk to you), that you now put yourself in the customers' shoes.

How about compiling a list of the attributes and behaviour of the person you would like to look after you in a retail outlet? How do you want to be treated? List below six key points:

1	
2	
3	
4	
5	
6	

Here are my recommendations (and it will be great if your list and mine are similar):

- A smiling face. This should be genuine. We have all been told that people buy more with their eyes than they do with their ears. If you were welcoming a friend into your house, you would quite naturally smile. It is also pleasurable when walking into someone else's premises to be greeted with a smile. If you are lazy this should appeal, as apparently it takes less muscle power to smile than it does to frown.

- Eye contact. It is so important to look people in the eyes. Not only do you convey body language when you look someone in the eye but you also are subconsciously registering that person's body language. We have become conditioned to believe that a person who looks us in the eyes is more trustworthy.

- Be pleased to see the customer. This is harder to describe, but it is a combination of facial expression, body language and tone of voice. We have all experienced, at some time or another, sales people who give us the impression that we are a nuisance and are interrupting their day. This really is irritating when we as customers, should we make a purchase, are actually making a contribution to their pay packet. I have often longed to say 'I help to keep you employed, so be nice to me.'

- Don't pounce! I have already said that the majority of us have difficulty with pushy sales people, and there is a balance between pouncing and being hard to get. Remember the role in retail selling is not only to help people choose the right product, but it is also to give them an enjoyable experience. It is of course necessary to make some form of greeting – to acknowledge their presence. The classic greeting is 'Can I help you?', which easily solicits the response 'No, thank you, I am just looking.' The improvement is 'How can I help you?' In some instances another polite greeting may be 'Is there anything that you are looking for?' Either of the aforementioned gets a better response with the smiling face and the enthusiastic positive tone of voice. You will of course still get a response from time to time of customers saying 'I just want to have a look around, thank you.' It is then very professional to follow that reply with any of the following: 'Fine', 'Great', 'You are most welcome' or 'My name is… If you would like any information or assistance I would be very pleased to help you.'

- Introduce yourself. When customers tell you what they are looking for or how you may help them, introduce yourself. In big-ticket selling (cars, white goods, furniture, etc) it is then correct for you to get your customers' names and to use those names in conversation. 'My name is… I'm sorry, I don't know your name.' Always address the customer as Mr or Ms but introduce yourself only by your first name.

- Ask questions. This is the most important selling skill, and I will be continually reminding you throughout the book. The most successful sales people are the ones who master the skills of finding out by asking questions about exactly what the customer is looking for. Of course, in many cases customers may be unsure of what they are looking for, but nevertheless the good sales person can help the customer by asking the right questions. For example, for a customer looking for a dishwasher, the sales person could ask the question 'Are you on a water meter?', because the customer may not be aware that there are some machines that use less water than others. Consider your own experience of having been frustrated by a sales person who has endeavoured to sell you something that you didn't want. If only the sales person had had the courtesy to ask and get a very clear understanding of your requirements, the sale would have taken place smoothly and pleasurably.

- Don't oversell. This is another extremely irritating habit of poor sales people. They talk about the features of a product that are not of interest to you and in many cases get too technical and want to blind you with their knowledge and jargon. I personally am not a petrol head, but unfortunately I have to change my car from time to time and find it so irritating when sales people want to tell me about brake horsepower and engine torque. I am more interested in fuel economy, comfort, appearance and the sound system. But there are numerous car buyers who are deeply interested in engine torque, brake horsepower and 0 to 60 in five seconds. So find out by asking the right questions.

- The add-on. It is perfectly correct, thoroughly professional and in most cases in the customers' best interests to offer the add-on. But this must only be offered or suggested when the first sale is complete. What I mean by the add-on is an item that customers often don't think about, for example the shoe trees and polish that could go with a new pair of shoes, the extended warranty for a white-goods purchase, the paper to go with a new photocopier, or the printer to go with the digital camera. The list here is endless. The good sales person will always think on behalf of the customer. This is not pressurised selling but is giving your customers the chance to make the decision for themselves on items that perhaps they had not thought of or did not know existed.

- Product knowledge. Now this is so obvious and important, but it is all too common (and very irritating) to find that sales people lack knowledge of their products. No doubt you have experienced sales people, perhaps in one of the multiple electrical outlets, who have read the information off the display card, as opposed to imparting accurate information about the product that you may be interested in. I will be covering this in more detail in Chapter 6. To sum up, enthusiasm from a sales person is infectious. The balance is not to be gushing, not to be creepy, but to be genuinely enthusiastic about your products or services.

Telephone enquiries

These calls come from a variety of sources. They can be via advertising, recommendations, websites, PR, directories and mailshots. It is therefore important to know that your customers have choice and that their call to you may be one of a number of enquiries that they are making. Statistically, 85 per cent of calls coming into a business are customer related. The others are a mixture of personal calls and calls from supply companies. Therefore, it is essential to answer the phone quickly, ideally by the third ring. The greeting should be welcoming. Answer the phone with your company's name. Smile when you answer the phone, as this alters your tone of voice. A smile can be heard over the phone. Enquire as to the person's name, but please don't say 'Who's calling?' It is far better to say 'May I have your name, please?' Best of all, if the call is from an existing customer, is to recognise the voice and use the customer's name immediately.

Once you have the person's name, introduce yourself. It is so much easier and nicer for customers to have the name of the person that they are talking to. Do listen carefully to the enquiry. If you are in any doubt, ask again, for example 'Do I understand correctly? Are you looking for…?' If you then have to pass callers to someone else, always give the name of the person you are putting them through to and make sure that they are connected. If there is any difficulty in connecting callers, get their telephone number, promise to call back and state when the return call will be made.

Now if you are able to handle the enquiry yourself and can complete the sale over the phone it is just as important and in many cases more so to offer the add-on, as described in the previous section on retail selling. In many cases customers can be so focused on the one product that they forget or are not aware of the add-ons. There are of course occasions when there is an opportunity to 'up-sell'.

This basically means offering a better product than the one the customer was enquiring about. There also may be an opportunity to cross-sell by offering a new or different product that you may have available. For example, 'Mr/Ms Customer, you may or may not be aware that we also do…'

E-mail enquiries

E-mail and the internet are a vital element of business and a brilliant sales tool. It must be accepted that e-mail enquiries can happen 24 hours a day. But the rule of thumb is to respond quickly with the information requested. If customers place an order – and put yourself in their shoes here – they will want confirmation that the order has been received, and they will want dispatch information as well. May I remind you that every enquiry could lead to a customer becoming a brand ambassador? If you are unable to meet their request, how about (1) offering an alternative or even (2) recommending a competitor? It is fascinating where this can lead you in the future. I personally recommend, as we do in our office, that on the back of an e-mail enquiry you always endeavour to speak to the customer. This does prove that in many cases business can be won as one gleans more information from customers as to the problem they have that they need to solve. Most sales result from a customer problem. Remember, as I stated in the Introduction, you are a solutions specialist.

Shows and exhibitions

Primarily, there are two activities that relate to shows and exhibitions. First is actively selling products off the stand. It is obvious that the display of the merchandise should look attractive and well presented. However, the behaviour of the seller often leaves a lot to be desired. We have all seen sales people sitting behind their goods looking miserable, reading a newspaper or magazine and/or stuffing their face with food. Sales people should be standing. They should be smiling and looking happy. They should be making eye contact. They should be looking busy even if they are just rearranging the merchandise. They should show enthusiasm about their products if the customer wishes to engage in conversation.

Do always allow customers to touch and to handle the merchandise. It is a well-known fact that when people handle a product they are more likely to buy.

The second activity relates more to trade shows and exhibitions. This is primarily in the B2B sector. Very rarely is money exchanged here and only occasionally are orders placed. The purpose of the trade show or exhibition is to get leads, which can be followed up at a later date. The layout of the stands is of paramount importance. It must be possible for a customer on approaching the stand to understand within five seconds exactly what you do and what you are selling. Far too many trade stands are littered with verbiage that the prospective customer will not stop to read. So it must be very, very simple. Another major mistake that is made by many exhibitors is concentrating their efforts into sticking brochures into prospective customers' hands. Many trade shows give their attendees plastic bags on arrival to collect the literature rubbish, the majority of which will go straight in the bin after people leave. This of course makes good profits for the printers, designers and paper manufacturers but virtually nil for the exhibitor. My recommendation, when customers genuinely want a brochure or literature, is to explain to them, as we do, that you have run out but if they give you a business card or contact details you will get a brochure or literature in the post to them. This process eliminates an enormous amount of wasted time, and anyone who is genuinely interested will of course give their contact information.

You can measure the success of a show or exhibition by how many enquiries or leads you obtain. It is therefore imperative not only to mail out information requested but also to enclose a covering letter stating that you will phone within the next two or three days (1) to make sure that the enquirer has received the information and (2) to turn the enquiry into a meeting.

Internet

The internet is extremely important for virtually every business, and there are many specialists who have massive expertise in not only the design of a website but also how to maximise exposure on the various search engines. Websites have the sole purpose of getting customers either to place an order by e-mail or to telephone their enquiry through. All of this is covered in the earlier sections of this chapter, but it is not the purpose of this book to discuss the detail of selling via the web. We can recommend some outstandingly good business specialists in this area. For help contact success@denny.co.uk

Key Questions

- Do I always smile on meeting a customer?

- Do I look customers in the eye?

- Do I ask pertinent and suitable questions?

- Do I have good product knowledge about the products I am selling?

- Do I answer the phone by the third ring?

- Do I respond immediately to an enquiry?

Selling out-house

The telephone call; The letter; E-mail; Voicemail;
Some tips on making excellent telephone calls

As opposed to selling in-house, selling out-house involves the sales person going to the potential customer's premises. This can be divided into two main categories: B2B, in other words business transacted on business premises, and home sales, ie business transacted in the home.

The main purpose of this chapter is to give advice for the sales person to get B2B appointments. I am not going to cover appointment making for home sales, as most of these are not cold appointments. They start with an enquiry and then the sales person makes the appointment on the back of the enquiry. I will, however, cover just one or two key points that are very important for those readers who are involved in home sales.

First, you are at people's homes at the invitation of the householders. Put yourself in their shoes. They quite probably have been looking forward to the appointment but nevertheless are almost certainly sceptical and in many cases possibly even cynical. When they answer the door, immediately there is an interaction. They will judge the sales person's appearance not only by how he or she is dressed but by hairstyle, facial expression and what the sales person is carrying. It is therefore essential that the seller encourages immediate confidence, and trust, by how they present themselves. This will be covered in more detail in Chapter 5.

When the sales person is invited in there could well be distractions of children and/or pets. This is not an excuse for the sales person to be artificial or creepy, but it is certainly acceptable to be polite, to acknowledge their existence and to use their names if the householder discloses them. In many home sales there could be two people involved, either husband and wife or two partners. Please never make the mistake of assuming that one of them is the decision maker. Don't address just one individual; speak to both and have eye contact with both customers. If you are going to sit down, never sit between the two; they should be sitting together. All the rest of your presentation and communication will be covered in the following chapters.

Making Appointments in B2B Selling

Stage One

Making appointments for B2B is possibly one of the most loathed jobs for sales people but nevertheless is one of the most important. This has often been termed 'cold calling'. In the past it used to be cost-effective to go door-knocking, but this is definitely not the case in the current economic climate. We have covered in Chapter 2 how to find the people you wish to sell to, so you should be concentrating your efforts on that list. Finding people will be referred to as stage one.

Stage Two

You must now decide whether to make your first approach by telephone, letter or even possibly e-mail.

The telephone call

If you are comfortable with making the cold calls – fantastic. Here is a basic outline script, but this must be varied according to your customer profile.

You dial the company. The switchboard answers. All you should say is 'Richard Jones, please' (the name of the person you wish to speak to). You will be asked 'Who's calling?' Give your first and last name but not your company. If the receptionist asks for your company name, of course pass this on. You will then be put through to the individual or to his or her PA. Again, just say 'Richard Jones, please'. You may be asked your company name and what your call is in connection with. Now this is where you must use your own words, but you could say 'I have been asked to give him a call by…' Or you could say 'We have a new… that I understand he might be interested in.'

If you are speaking to Richard Jones himself, introduce yourself by stating your name, your company and what you do. 'What you do' should be about the result, not the product or service itself. For example, you could say 'We increase productivity for our clients' or 'We increase our customers' profitability.' In other words, make a statement that gets the other person thinking 'That sounds interesting.' This statement should be no longer than 15 seconds.

> *'So, Mr Jones, the purpose of my call is to see if it's possible for us to meet for 10 or 15 minutes so that I can explain very briefly what we do.'*

The letter

Writing a letter has one purpose only and that is to sell a follow-up telephone call, which in turn will later sell the appointment. Here are some sample letters.

> *Ms J Smith*
> *Job title*
> *Company name*
> *Address*
>
> *Dear Ms Smith*
>
> *May I introduce myself and my company/firm to you?*

The purpose of this letter is to inform you that we have one or two new developments within our product/service/range that may be of interest to you.

I obviously have no idea at this stage if this is the case, so I will be telephoning you within the next two or three days to see if we may be able to fix up a very short meeting where I can explain in more detail.

I really look forward to speaking to you.

Yours sincerely

Signature

Name (typed)
Job title

Joe Bloggs
Joe Bloggs Associates
24 Market Way
Chipsdean
Westmanshire
CH2 8BL

Dear Joe

You may have heard that… are now delivering 'THE best value for money… services in the UK' – not our quote, but one from our customers.

The purpose of this letter is to see if we can arrange a very short meeting for you to see whether what we are currently able to achieve may be of interest to Joe Bloggs Associates, now or in the future.

I will phone you in the next two to three days to see when we could have a 20- to 25-minute get-together.

Yours sincerely

Signature

Name (typed)
Job title

PS In most cases we can guarantee to reduce costs, improve service and simplify administration.

Ms J Smith
Job title
Company name
Address

Dear Ms Smith

The purpose of writing to you is to introduce myself and my company.

We specialise in… and I believe some of our products/services could well be of interest. I also believe that they might save/make you a great deal of money.

I obviously have no idea whether this may be of interest, so I shall give you a call within the next two or three

SELLING OUT-HOUSE

days to see if we can arrange a very short meeting.

Yours sincerely

Signature

Name (typed)
Job title

It is very important to be aware that it is not easy to get appointments with decision makers. Their time is at a premium, and it is pointless in having a meeting with someone who is not a decision maker. Having sent the letter we go to stage three.

Stage Three

Stage three is the follow-up telephone call. This is also an activity that many people dislike, and the only reason for this dislike or dread is the fear of rejection. The other person might say 'I'm too busy' or 'No, I'm not interested.' Realistically, this isn't too bad anyhow.

So here is the process. Dial up the company and go through the same procedure that we had on the cold call until you are connected to your contact.

> *'Hello, Mr Smith. This is [your name] of [your company name]. Is it convenient to speak for a couple of minutes?'*
>
> *'Did you get my letter?'*
>
> *'The purpose of calling you, as I said in my letter, is that we have one or two products or services that may be of great interest to you. But I really have no idea at this stage, and in order to save a great deal of time may I suggest that we arrange a short meeting at your convenience? I don't know if you have your diary handy, but would 10.20 next Thursday be convenient, or some time the following week?'*

There are some key points in this process:

1. Do not attempt to sell or discuss your products or services in detail on the telephone. If they can be sold on the phone, why do you want an appointment? If you must talk about your products or services talk only about the results. But, best of all, leave this area alone.

2. Do not make a statement that you cannot justify.

3. Do not offer an appointment on the hour, as it appears that you could be there for one hour.

4. Do not offer an appointment on the half-hour as this implies a half-hour meeting.

5. Always choose an unusual time, as this implies that the meeting will be short. I will state it once again: a decision maker's time is precious. So why would he or she want to meet a complete stranger and give that person one hour out of his or her own bank account of time?

6. If your prospect says 'Can't you put something in the post?', the common-sense approach is to say 'The purpose

of me wishing to see you is so that I can leave you with only the information that you would be really interested in. Apart from that, Ms Smith, I would really like to meet you.'

7. It really is important to understand that it is very unlikely that you will come out of a first meeting, that to all intents and purposes is a cold call, with an order. If you do, it will be luck – just being in the right place at the right time. The most important objective of this approach is to start a relationship that will eventually lead to a sale.

E-mail

This is becoming increasingly intrusive, and I do not recommend the cold approach via e-mail, with the following exception. If you have your contact's e-mail address you could send the following message:

> ***Attention Mary Jones. I will be calling you tomorrow between 10.00 and 2.00 as we have... that may be of interest to you. The purpose of***

my telephone call will be to see if we can arrange a 10- or 15-minute meeting at your convenience.

People have often asked me whether it really is effective to travel a long way for such a short meeting, and in my experience with every sales organization that I have been involved with the answer is 'Yes'. It is far better for both the customer and the sales person's usage of time to have a short meeting where

1. the outcome will be a 'No, thank you'

2. if there is real interest the meeting could extend and lead to either a sale or a second meeting

3. (and this is the same as number 1) of course the outcome could be a 'No, not today'

Voicemail

There is an increased use of voicemail, which we are all experiencing. When you are following up a letter and are confronted with voicemail you have two choices: either leave a message or phone again. My advice is to call again, as it is pretty useless asking your recipient to return your call. In my experience only the very best business people return calls. It appears that weak and poorly organised individuals do not. My final suggestion is to try phoning outside normal business hours or get the mobile telephone number of your contact from the switchboard or secretary.

This can be difficult, so here is a tip. When asking for a mobile number try this phraseology:

> *'Can you help me, please? I promised Ms Smith that I would call her. We seem to be missing each other. Have you got a mobile number that I can make contact with her on?'*

Some tips on making excellent telephone calls

1. Always smile while you are speaking on the telephone. It does project a better telephone manner.

2. Be enthusiastic. Enthusiasm is very infectious.

3. Always plan your call before you pick up the phone.

4. Decide exactly what you want to achieve before you dial.

5. Have the courtesy to put yourself in the recipient's shoes.

Key Questions

- Would I buy from me?
- Do I plan my calls?
- Do I have a system for regularly sending letters?
- Do I set a daily time to make outgoing calls?

5

Planning and preparation

Prepare yourself for sales meetings; Product knowledge; Read the person; Speak slowly; Time; Goals and targets; Rehearse

It is fairly obvious but nevertheless worth stating that people prefer to buy from people they like. In most cases our customers have massive choice, as you do. I suggest that you probably currently do business with people that you like and trust and probably have built up confidence with over a period of time. You could possibly buy better or more cheaply, but probably there are some people that you just will not do business with because you don't like them. That emotional feeling may be caused by the way that they communicated to you or by a lack of trust that could be conveyed by body language or what they said – or perhaps even by their reputation.

A great proportion of buying choice is based upon an emotion. It is therefore essential to build trust and confidence. Being personable of course is a big advantage in selling, and like most behaviours it can be learned. Let me remind you: people don't buy from companies; they buy from people. Research has shown that in 84 per cent of sales situations it is emotion and not logic that persuades people to buy. What normally happens is that people buy on emotional grounds and then justify that decision on logic. Logic is nevertheless extremely important but has little persuasive power. I'll bet you can think of numerous sales people who should have gone to charm school, and though charm is extremely difficult to describe it should certainly include kindness and courtesy.

My wife, Dorothy, teases me when she claims (and she's probably right) that my favourite word is 'balance'. I have heard people talk about integrity and savoir-faire, but it is all a question of balance. However, too much integrity can appear to be blunt, and too much savoir-faire can be creepy. To me, kindness and courtesy are about being genuinely interested in other people and what you can do for them rather than what they can do for you.

PLANNING AND PREPARATION

Most of this book is designed to help sales people sell out of house. There are of course many techniques that will also apply to in-house selling. When the sales person walks in to meet a prospective customer, the customer may have an open mind or may have some expectations, but in most cases that first impression is all-important. Appearances do count. The sales person's appearance should be in tune with the product or service. If you are selling tractors to farmers it is completely out of order to wear a city suit with city shoes. On the other hand, such attire will be acceptable for a lawyer, accountant, or someone selling consultancy or training. If the appearance is in tune with the product, confidence can rise and the door to trust will be opened.

Your customers no doubt will be asking themselves subconsciously 'I wonder if this person and this company are any good? I wonder if I can trust them and rely on them to look after my needs. And I wonder if they will do what they say they are going to do?' In most situations, if you are selling out of house, often called field sales, to customers, you are the company. You might be the only contact or you might be the main contact for them. Their thoughts are really in your control. Being in control is every sales person's dream and requires planning and preparation.

Prepare yourself for sales meetings

Most sales people do actually do this, but they often make the mistake of planning the agenda. They plan what they are going to say and what they want to discuss. A far better approach is to plan what you would like your prospect to give you during the meeting:

1. the contract or order

2. the information that you would like to take away

3. a date or time when the sale could be possible or when the prospect might need your product or service

4. a date for the next meeting

5. details of other people involved in the decision-making process

6. information about who the prospect's current suppliers are

7. information about who made the decision to select the current supplier

8. information about what the prospect's buying criteria are, including price and value for money. This is just a start. So now compile your own list of information that you wish to gain from this first meeting. Fascinatingly, this helps in planning the agenda

It is common sense but, as we all know, common sense is not too common. Prior to the meeting, have you done some homework on the company? This is made easy with access to the internet. Part of the planning and preparation for meetings should also entail you having examples of similar companies that you have done or do work with, and one sure way of building confidence is with case histories. In many cases, these may not be shown at the first meeting but almost certainly should be shown at a subsequent meeting. This is one of the most powerful techniques of persuasiveness and convincing others that is still underutilised. We see it in play in advertising where personalities endorse a product or tell their story of what that product did for them. Yes, I do accept that we have become a little sceptical about personalities and their endorsements, but real-life case histories in B2B are very powerful.

Product knowledge

Having good knowledge of your products does not mean only that you know how they are made, what they consist of and the technical data; it is much more important that you know what your products actually do. And what they can do must be presented in a way that is of interest to the prospective customer. Jargon and abbreviations should be used only when you know for certain that your prospect understands and/or uses similar phraseology.

Read the person

Really professional sales people realise the importance of body language, so I recommend that if you are unfamiliar with this subject you read up on it. Apparently there are 750,000 body language signals. There are

15,000 from the face alone. When the spoken word is in conflict with the body language, the body language will be the true reflection of thought. Most people know that you mustn't get too close to introverted people, who need more space. You can often pick this up subconsciously by their handshake or by the way they sit down and push the chair slightly backwards. More extroverted people will draw the chair up under them or slightly forward. I mention this only so that you will be aware of and build your own understanding of body language, as it is not my intention to cover it in detail in this book.

Speak slowly

Enthusiasm is essential and infectious but is not an excuse for speaking too quickly. From the customer's or prospect's viewpoint, a person speaking too quickly does not build trust, whereas individuals who take time and think carefully about what they are going to say will build confidence and trust.

Time

I am often asked whether there is a right or wrong time to sell. I have never come up with any research that shows the best time to sell. My experience shows there are definitely wrong times, and this again is really common sense: when a person is in a hurry for another engagement, when a person's body language shows that they are under stress or pressure, or if the person says emphatically 'Now is not a good time.' Most of these examples have nothing to do with time of day. However, how you use your time is crucial to your overall sales. We have already covered how much of your total working time (TWT) is spent in communication with customers. Customer contact time (CCT) is your measure of eventual sales achievement. It is completely normal that sales people can convince themselves that a certain time of day is not good for making a sales presentation or having a meeting. From my whole life's experience I can honestly say that I think this is rubbish. I have had good sales meetings at 8.00 in the morning and at 8.00 at night and on a Monday and on a Friday, so just don't allow yourself to believe that there is a right or wrong time of day.

Goals and targets

Every successful sales person is goal or target driven. Most targets are set by the company's management, and most successful sales managers set targets that are achievable. But you can set your own targets that may be in excess of those that you are given. It is a common characteristic of successful people to have goals, whether conscious or subconscious. These goals don't relate just to business achievement. It is even more important to have goals for your private life. The purpose of business activity is to enable you to achieve your personal goals. It is proven that you will be more likely to achieve your personal goals if they are clearly identified, possibly written in your diary, but crucially visualised.

I mention a diary because this helps to plan and focus the mind. There is something very motivational about seeing a diary with meetings booked not only for the week or month ahead but also for next year. I refer to these, as they could be on the back of a 'No, not today'.

In my book **Selling to Win**, I describe in detail the most effective time management system for sales people. Just one very useful tip here: at the end of each day plan and put in your diary your 'to do' list for the following day. Never make your list at the beginning of the working day; it should be made at the end of the previous day. Planning and goal setting will inevitably help you to achieve your sales targets, and the result without question will be greater income. Take a leaf out of every Olympian's book. Planning and training start at least four years prior to the big event.

Rehearse

There is of course a lot more to planning and preparation, from diary management to effective time planning, that it is not necessary to cover in detail, but part of your planning to be an effective sales person should embrace mental rehearsal. Top athletes and individual sports superstars from golfers to tennis players and snooker players spend 70 per cent of their working life in practice or training. But prior to the event they will mentally rehearse and build in their mind a positive picture of what they want the outcome to be. If they allow themselves to picture in their mind a failure that will inevitably become the result. We are only just starting to learn the enormous power and potential of the human brain. You have one. How are you going to use yours?

Key Questions

- Do I build trust when I meet people?
- Does my appearance build confidence?
- Do I decide before every meeting what I want?
- Do I have suitable case histories?
- Have I read up on body language?
- Have I got sales targets that I believe in?

- Do I always finish the day by planning the next day with a 'to do' list?

- Do I know what I want to be achieving four years from today?

(6)

Sales expertise

Sell yourself; Ask the right questions; Listen well; Link features and benefits Sell the results; Identify your unique sales points (USPs); Don't knock the competition; Understand buying emotions; Listen and learn; Names and detail; It's not what you say; Be positive; Self-motivation

This book is about how to be successful at selling; it is not just about learning selling 'skills'. If you are going to take up any activity, why not strive to be the best? The rewards can be mind-blowing.

This chapter is mostly common sense but demonstrates the characteristics and principles of very good sales people, the winners, as against the also-rans. I am continually asked by journalists: what is new in selling or what new innovative techniques are sales people practising these days? I have to say every time: not a lot. Of course, sales people have to adapt to changing markets, competition, and new ways of trading, but fundamentally people are really just the same. Consumers don't like some new gimmicky technique that gets them to buy something that they didn't really want or need.

In this chapter we are going to run through some of the foundation principles that build sales expertise.

Sell yourself

Most of us have been told to sell ourselves at school or university by a careers adviser, but very few people have been taught how to sell themselves. Does this mean we have to talk about ourselves? Does this mean we have to be egotistical? The answer is the opposite in most cases. When people go for a job interview they are expected to talk about themselves, and this is normally encouraged by the interviewer asking the right questions. But the successful candidates are the ones who naturally are comfortable but do not labour the point and spend too much time talking about all of their jobs, qualifications and life story. What they do is to show interest not only in the job vacancy but in the company and possibly the interviewer.

Selling yourself is therefore not about talking about yourself but about being interested in the other person. If you are a sales person it is an absolute no-no to talk about yourself in more than a sentence, and that should be primarily for the purpose of credibility. You may say something like 'I have been with this company for only three months so there may be some points that I cannot answer for you' or 'I have been with this company for five years and in that time I have experienced most situations that you are likely to come across.'

It is far better to be humble but demonstrate your knowledge and experience by the anecdotes and stories that you share.

Ask the right questions

Yes, here it is again. This is the single most important selling skill, and I can honestly say that throughout my career the sales I should have won but lost were due to not asking the right questions.

Let me remind you of what I said earlier. Modern professional selling is termed 'consultative selling', and I hope that you like the term 'solution specialist' of a modern-day business winner. Now, you can only provide an effective solution if you have got all – and I mean all – the right information. Many readers will naturally be questioning this from the point of view of 'Well, I didn't win the sale because of price.' This will be covered in detail in Chapter 9.

I can't teach you the right questions, because all companies and products are different, but let me give you some ideas. You can preface all of the following who, what, why, when, where, how and which questions with a lead-in such as:

'Do you mind me asking...?'

'May I ask...?'

'Can I find out...?'

Here is a list of possible questions:

A list of 'who' questions:
- *'Who are your major competitors within your specific marketplace?'*

- *'Who are the prime users of the system?'*
- *'Who will require training?'*
- *'Who benefits from the data reports produced?'*
- *'Who compiles your data at the moment?'*

A list of 'what' questions:

- *'What would happen if…?'*
- *'What are you looking for in a software package?'*
- *'What access do you require?'*
- *'What can we do to make this happen?'*
- *'What skills will be required to achieve the result?'*

A list of 'why' questions:

- *'Why do you produce these reports at the moment?'*
- *'Why do you need…?'*
- *'Why do you think that?'*

- 'Why will you need more time?'
- 'Why do you do that?'

A list of 'when' questions:

- 'When are you looking to implement this system?'
- 'When is a good time to discuss…?'
- 'When will you be getting your new budgets?'
- 'When is a good time to start the programme?'
- 'When will be more convenient?'

A list of 'where' questions:

- 'Where will the… be located?'
- 'Where does your analysis come from at present?'
- 'Where is the money coming from?'
- 'Where is it going to be located?'

A list of 'how' questions:

- *'How important is this project to you?'*
- *'How quickly do you require the…?'*
- *'How many people will be required?'*
- *'How can we progress further with this?'*

A list of 'which' questions:

- *'Which is more important to you?'*
- *'Which colour is going to be most suitable?'*
- *'Which one is your favourite?'*
- *'Which system do you think is going to be right for you?'*

That last section of 'which' questions is often most utilised in the closing of a sale. Most sales training techniques describe this as the 'choice' close. It is a way of focusing the prospect's mind that can usually lead to a sale completed.

Let me share with you my favourite question of all. This is appropriate in the situation where the sales person has done everything that appears to be right, the parties have had many meetings, and there appears to be a friendly relationship, but there is no business, order or sale. Now this is the great question:

> *'Mr/Ms..., what have I got to do in order to do business with you?'*

Listen well

The sales person who is skilled at asking the right questions and listening carefully to what the prospect or customer has said will find that most people give numerous buying signals. You learn more by listening than ever by talking. The also-rans of the sales world think that they are listening, but what they are really doing is thinking about what they are going to say next. Hopefully you have two ears and one mouth, and that is the ratio by which they should operate. You can listen to what has been said as well as listen to what has not been said. If you are in any doubt about what the customer is saying or asking, go for clarification. Don't ever assume. You have no doubt heard the definition: assuming makes an ass- out of u- and -me.

ASS-U-ME

An enquiry about a price is a buying signal. An enquiry about a delivery date is a buying signal. An enquiry about colour or style is a buying signal. Listening – really listening – to what people say and sometimes even repeating back for clarification will build trust and will win you more business.

Please don't ever ignore a buying signal. This demonstrates that your customer is genuinely interested. If you can satisfy the buying signal you are in a position to close the sale.

Link features and benefits

All products and services have what are described as features and benefits. The feature is the detail of what the product or service consists of. Let's take the example of a motor car. This car has front and rear parking sensors, an on-board computer and satellite navigation.

It is of course important to mention them, but best of all to do so as an excuse to describe the benefits:

'This vehicle has front and rear parking sensors, which means that you are less likely to damage your car when parking. This model has an on-board computer, which means that it will tell you when you need your next service, so you don't have to worry about it. It will also tell you what your fuel consumption is and provides you with a travel log among many other features. Satellite navigation is standard, which means that you don't have to struggle with maps in a lay-by or worry about getting lost or having to ask someone for directions.'

You will notice I have used the link phrase 'which means that'. Don't overuse this phrase, but it is a very useful reminder to talk not just about features. If you are under pressure for time in a sales meeting, talk about the benefits. They are more important than the features.

Sell the results

Don't sell your products. Sell the results of what your product or service will do. There is a very big difference here. You've seen the advertisements for make-up. What they are selling is the beauty. Toothpaste is sold on the basis of white teeth. The old sales person's adage is to sell the sizzle not the steak.

Identify your unique sales points (USPs)

This is really essential if your product or service is in competition with others. Every business and every product or service has something that is unique. Knowing what this is and then how to use it will certainly help you to win sales when you are up against tough competition.

First, ask yourself: why should customers buy your product or service when they could get something similar from someone else? What is so special about your product or service? Too often, sales people base their uniqueness on price and, as you will see in Chapter 9, this is not always the customer's reason for purchasing. Let me repeat: every product or service does have something unique. It may be delivery. It may be speciality. It may be selection of colours, varieties, past experience in the marketplace, the position of your premises, or one of a number of other things.

Complete the 3 sections below by entering any points that you feel are unique to your product or service, your company and yourself.

1. Product or service

_____

2. My company

_____

3. Myself

_____

Having identified your USPs it is then necessary to find out if they are of interest or importance to your customer. Remember, modern-day selling is not about telling but asking:

'Would it be of interest... for you to deal with someone who...?'

'Would it be important... for you that the company that you select has...?'

Now build up your own list of questions. If your prospect attaches an importance to or declares a strong interest in your USPs, you are diminishing the value of the competition.

Don't knock the competition

This should be common sense, but sadly it is a habit that many weak sales people resort to in endeavouring to win a sale. You don't know, but possibly your prospects have previously purchased from the competition, and it was their decision to do so. Equally it is important not to fear your competitors' products or prices. If you show concern, your customer will pick up the vibes and will lose confidence in you.

I am often asked my opinion about other companies that provide training or executive recruitment, which is our core business. I handle this by smiling immediately, which helps to develop a comfortable relationship, and then pass a fairly bland statement, without criticism, but the tone of voice diminishes the value or importance of the other companies.

In many sales situations your customer will be inviting presentations or quotations from others, no doubt as you would do, if you were having some improvements to your home for instance. If your customer discloses this, ask in the politest way possible who you are up against. Now, by using your industry knowledge, steal their thunder. Explain your competitors' USPs, because they will if you don't. When the time comes for the competitors to release their USPs, they will have less impact.

Understand buying emotions

There is a lot of talk about emotional intelligence, which covers such topics as empathy, initiative, adaptability and persuasiveness. These behavioural traits have always been important in the make-up of really good sales people, and so it is important for you to make sure that you have a really good understanding of your own strengths and weaknesses. That is in your control.

Now what about the buyer? What are the emotions behind buying decisions? Research carried out by the Harvard Business School has shown that 84 per cent of all buying decisions are based on emotion and not logic. The buyer makes a decision based on emotion and then justifies that decision on logical grounds. You must be aware of these two factors in the decision, because they are usually present and usually powerful. It is said that people will always find the money for the things that they really want but don't necessarily need, while at the same time they may need a product or service but not necessarily want it. You know where the money will go.

The fear of loss and the desire of gain are two very powerful driving emotions. Most people fear loss more than they desire gain. Let me give you an example. If you mislay a £10 note you will put in an inordinate amount of effort to try to find it, but do you put the same effort into earning an extra £10?

There are occasions when this knowledge is very important and can be part of the sales person's armoury, not for the purpose of making customers buy something that they don't want or need but to help customers come to a decision. One very acceptable and highly ethical way of communicating with the understanding that emotion is involved but logic will get the decision to stay firm is to communicate via stories. Now I don't mean made-up stories. It is imperative that you tell stories best described as case histories or stories that your customers have told you about their experiences. This is a very powerful form of persuasive communication, because the stories will illustrate the results of either your or the competitors' products or services.

Listen and learn

The vast majority of successful sales people have listened to more successful sales people than themselves. They have learned the techniques, phraseology and work ethic and then put them into practice. Find out from the most successful sales people in your company or industry what they do; don't do what the also-rans do and that is to justify their inadequacies by saying 'It's all right for them but…' Make sure that you mix with and meet successful people, as all of us are conditioned by our environment.

Names and detail

Some people are naturally good at recalling a person's name, but others have to work at it. The sweetest sound in the whole of the human language is the sound of our own name. There are many techniques for developing this skill, and it really does build confidence and trust when you can recall not only the other person's name but also some detail that the person may have shared with you. One little tip that could well be of help - after you have been introduced you might say, 'I'm sorry, I didn't catch your name' and then repeat the person's name. People never feel embarrassed if they have to repeat their name. This also demonstrates that you consider the person to be of importance and that his or her name is also important.

It's not what you say

Most of us have heard the expression 'It's not what you say but how you say it.' When we are training people on telephone techniques either to sell on the phone or to handle customer enquiries and so on, we emphasise that the tone of the voice, in most cases, is more important than the actual words. Many people have a certain telephone manner when telephoning family, friends and people they know fairly well but in a business context seem to observe a different code. So, whether you are on the phone or face to face, be an interesting person, which can very easily be achieved by the movement in your voice. In other words, do not communicate in a monotone or at a single level. Sound enthusiastic but of course not too over the top. On other occasions you may have to lower your voice and sound really concerned, for example if a customer needs help or is complaining.

Be positive

Expect the best. Don't live in the past. Live today and for the future. Be positive in what you say to others and just as importantly what you say to yourself: the 'I can' as against the 'I can't', the successes against the failures. Continually challenge yourself. Are you expecting to win or are you expecting to lose?

Self-motivation

If you ask sales people whether they are motivated they will usually reply 'Of course I am.' If you follow that question with 'How often?' you will get an uncomfortable reaction. Motivation is an important aspect of selling and can dramatically affect the behaviour of any individual at any moment. Most companies and sales people claim that motivation is important yet seem to do very little to foster it. Well, sales people shouldn't blame their employers, which is why this section is headed 'Self-motivation'. Sales people shouldn't rely upon their manager, the lucky sales call, the advertising, or even a sunny day to enhance their motivation.

Motivation has to come from within rather than from you hoping that someone else will do it for you. You build your motivation by always having something that you look forward to doing or having. Most successful sales people are ambitious and competitive. They have goals and targets that they wish to achieve. They have goals and ambitions in their private, social and recreational life. They are driven by the opportunity of winning and enhancing their standard of living. So, self-motivation really is available to all. It is the acceptance and understanding that your brain will deliver if it knows what is expected of it. It is all very well for me in this book to share with you skills and techniques of selling, but I challenge you:

how badly or strongly do you want to be a successful sales person? It is not in the knowing but in the doing, and it is the self-motivation that culminates in the doing.

So now set your goals, your sales targets and where you would like to be and what you would like to be achieving in one year from today. Take charge of your own motivation and do whatever it takes to stay motivated.

Key Questions

- Do I talk about myself too much?
- Will I now prepare a list of questions prior to each sales meeting?
- Do I really concentrate when listening?
- Have I got a benefit for each of my products or services?
- Have I got stories that illustrate loss and gain?
- Do I work daily on positive thinking and self-motivation?
- Have I written down one sentence stating the results of my product or service?

The classic presentation

Stage one – getting yourself accepted; Stage two – getting attention; Stage three - asking the right questions; Stage four - checking; Stage five – the marriage; Stage six – the final check; Stage seven – the close

There is or should be a natural, ethical and decent way to conduct a sales meeting or, if you prefer, a sales presentation. For many years sales training was built around the sales presentation technique of **'AIDA'**:

A Attention
I Interest
D Desire
A Action

This, though absolutely correct, is a little bit simplistic and requires in modern-day communication to be taken into more detail. Every one of those points is of course important. Sales people must attract attention from their prospects. They must find out the prospects' interests – what it is that they want or need. The sales people should then increase the prospects' desire and then finally take the action of closing the sale.

The sales presentation I wish to share with you is the pure unadulterated theory of the classical sales presentation. You don't have to run through all seven stages every single time. Your experience will tell you where to start and the direction to proceed in. But unless you know and keep within the boundaries you will diminish your chances of being truly successful. There has been a common complaint from prospects and customers alike of sales people being either boring or, at worst, irrelevant and boring. This is caused by a complete lack of structure to a sales meeting, and the root cause of that is either no sales training or even worse useless cheap training from failed sales people.

Some sales people are able to present only with the aid of PowerPoint. This has become grossly overused and in most cases is ineffectual. It can be a brilliant tool, but only to illustrate items that are best presented visually, and it must be relevant to the prospective customer. I personally believe that the content is best kept to a minimum, and there definitely should not be line upon line of words.

There are seven stages to the presentation.

Stage one – becoming accepted

This is the time spent building a rapport and establishing some common ground – selling yourself as well as finding out about your prospect. Don't overdo this. Don't waste people's time. Read your prospect's body language and assess the type of person that you are dealing with. The objective here is for your prospect to gain trust and confidence and for you to demonstrate that you are the sort of person who the prospect would be comfortable doing business with.

Stage two – getting attention

I often call this 'the opening prime desire statement'. You must say something to elicit a positive response (even if it is subconscious) from your prospect. Get him or her to think '

I want to hear what you have to say.' It is important to note here that you must never make a statement that you cannot substantiate.

> *'Mr Prospect, we have some policies that could increase the security for you dramatically, but I have no idea at this stage so I need to find out a little more about you.'*

Here are two further examples, one of which we use in our own company:

> *'We have a training course that I believe will almost certainly increase your sales, but may I find out a little bit more about your business before explaining in detail?'*

> *'We have some new products that will probably get you more business, enhance profits and help you build a stronger customer base, but may I find out a little bit more about your business first?'*

Stage three – asking the right questions

This is the major part of any successful sales presentation. As I have said repeatedly, it requires forethought and planning. When you ask these questions make sure that you are absolutely certain that you understand the replies. It is equally important to note here that your questions should lead your prospect towards your USPs. This is what consultative selling is all about – finding out the how, why, what and where almost exactly as a physician would do. You are a solution specialist. It is perfectly acceptable to make notes here and is very professional. But, whatever you do, don't provide any solutions and don't do any selling at this stage.

Stage four – checking

This is really professional and it is acceptable to make sure you have got all of the relevant information. Make sure you are now aware of the prospective buyer's parameters. Here are a couple of examples:

'Ms Prospect, is there anything else that we have not discussed that you may be looking for?'

'Have I got all of the information or is there anything else that we have not touched on?'

In this check make sure you have talked about money – possibly not the exact prices but ensure at least that your prospect is aware of your prices. Let me remind you of a point that I mentioned earlier. Whenever you lose a sale that you should have won it will be because you did not ask the right questions and did not get all of the relevant information. There are certain mistakes that sales people make most commonly. They may not talk about money and find out about budgets, availability and money expectations. Sometimes the prospect may appear to be a decision maker but is not, and the sales person should have discovered this. Again, the sales person may not have realised that there was also a competitor bidding for the business.

Stage five – the marriage

At this stage and only at this stage you should start to sell. Sell your products, their features, and the benefits that relate to that prospect. Most importantly of all, make sure you are clearly describing the results. Only at this stage will you be able to provide the solutions. Sell your USPs, and equally don't tell them about features that will not interest them. Don't oversell. At this stage of the presentation, if you are given any buying signals or if your prospect indicates a willingness to proceed, stop selling and stop your presentation and close the sale. The also-rans just keep talking and end up by overselling and talking the prospect out of the sale.

I call this the marriage because we draw together your products or services and join them up with your prospect's problem, need or want.

Stage six – the final check

Ask your prospect a gentle question. Here are some examples:

'Mr Prospect, how does this sound to you from what we have discussed?'

'Ms Prospect, are you satisfied with what we have discussed?'

'Mr Prospect, we seem to have covered all of the points. Is there anything else we haven't looked at?'

'Is that OK?'

'Are you happy with that?'

While you were going through the marriage you should have visibly ticked off from your notes those points that you had listed as being important. The prospect will have seen the items being ticked off. So the check is there to make sure that your prospect is comfortable. Now if your client raises objections, which I prefer to call concerns (we will cover this in Chapter 8), basically this happens because you have not convinced the prospect of the benefits during the marriage. Sometimes this means that you have to backtrack.

Stage seven – the close

This really is a professional, decent and nice way of wrapping up the process. Over the years, sales training has developed an aura of mystery around closing techniques.

The closing of the sale really is not some special technique suddenly unleashed at the end of a presentation to persuade the unsuspecting to buy. The superstars of the sales world know that closing the sale begins in the first seconds of a meeting. Closing the sale, however, is a must in all selling environments. So here are some very straightforward ideas for you to follow, and it is so much easier if you have been following the classic presentation. Having checked at stage six and uncovered that the prospect is happy with what has been offered, you can say:

'Fine. Let's complete the paperwork.'

'Let's do the cheque now.'

Here are some more ideas. The first is called the choice close:

'Do you prefer to pay by cheque or cash?'

'Do you want red or green?'

'Do you want 12 or 13?'

Or you could use the minor-point close:

'Do you want metallic paint on the car?'

'Would you like a pair of shoe trees for your new shoes?'

'How many handbooks will you require with this course?'

The purpose of closing is to draw the meeting or meetings to a conclusion.

Key Questions

- Have I prepared an 'attention getter'?
- Do I talk about and discuss money at stage three?

THE CLASSIC PRESENTATION

- Do I regularly check if my prospect is happy with what I am saying?

- If I lose a sale do I analyse where I went wrong?

8

Objections to reassurance

Prevention is better than cure; Stage one – ask back; Stage two – agree and outweigh; Stage three – provide the answer

In virtually every presentation at some stage a prospect will raise an objection. I prefer to call this a concern or maybe even a worry. When prospects raise an objection or concern it is because they are unsure, they don't understand, they need clarification or they just aren't convinced.

Prevention is better than cure

I truly believe that people like buying and they like being sold to when it is done well. It is common sense to prevent objections rather than having to provide a solution. Selling should never be a boxing match in which the customer throws a punch with an objection and the seller counters with an answer that provokes the customer to throw another and so on.

Poor selling raises objections. If you find you are getting a lot of objections or concerns, the first place to start looking for remedies is with your presentation. It is, therefore common sense to address the objections that regularly occur from your prospect before stage five (the marriage). You can find out if those concerns are likely to arise during stage three (the asking the right questions stage).

Let's look at some examples with this in mind. Suppose that you ask your prospect at the questioning stage:

>   *'How important is the price to you,
>   or are you looking for value?'*

The prospect may reply:

>   *'Well, I have already had a price
>   from Fishman Contractors. Let's see
>   what you come up with.'*

You know that Fishman Contractors are always cheaper than you, so that when you come to the selling stage (stage five) you must build value into your price and really sell your USPs if you have discovered that they are of real interest. You must give the prospect very good logical and emotional reasons as to why he or she should pay more for your product or service.

You are a solutions specialist and therefore must develop an understanding and an ability to handle objections and concerns.

There are three stages in handling objections correctly:

- Ask back
- Agree and outweigh
- Provide the answer

Stage One – ask back

The first stage in handling an objection is to find out if what is being said is the real objection. You must be absolutely clear about what is being asked of you in order for you to be able to answer that concern. Let me give you an example:

'The price is too high.'

You cannot handle this, because you don't know what it really means. It could mean:

- Somebody else is cheaper.
- It's more expensive than the prospect thought.
- The prospect can't afford it.
- The prospect wants a discount.
- It is outside the prospect's budget.
- The prospect is not the decision maker.
- It is the prospect's job to reduce the price.
- The prospect doesn't really want it.

When the statement 'The price is too high' is voiced, it could mean any of the above, so you have to find out by asking back with a suitable question:

> *'In relation to what?'*
>
> *'How much is too much?'*
>
> *'May I ask you why you say that?'*
>
> *'That's an interesting point. May I ask you why you think that it is too high?'*

By asking back you will eventually get to the real objection, and only when you have found the real objection should you proceed to the second stage.

Stage Two – agree and outweigh

Now agreement does not mean saying 'Oh, yes, I quite agree with that.' This will almost certainly lose you the sale. You must agree with the prospect's thought process, ie the reasoning that led him or her towards the core objection. Here are some examples you could use:

> *'I can understand your reasoning for saying that, Ms Prospect, but*

it has since been proved that...'

'I used to think the same but I have since discovered...'

'It's interesting that you should say that, Mr Prospect. Some of my best customers used to think that as well but they have found...'

Let me repeat: you are agreeing with the thoughts and not the objection, and you can outweigh the objection with experience, results and performance. It is perfectly acceptable at this stage to bring out credibility through customer case histories.

Stage Three – provide the answer

This stage is really quite simple: provide a very good, logical and convincing answer, of the kind you would want to receive if you were in the prospect's shoes.

Whatever you do, do not make up an answer. If you don't know, it is highly acceptable to say that you don't know. You can of course say to your prospect 'I will get that information for you.' In many selling situations the prospect could well say 'Oh, that's OK, it's not really important.' But nevertheless always speak the truth and use customer objections as an opportunity to gather further knowledge, which will in turn enhance your confidence and ability to become a very good sales person.

Ask people in your company how they handle the objection that you have difficulty with. If you have no means of getting this, by all means contact us at success@denny.co.uk

Key Questions

- Have I got a list of the most common objections?

- Have I asked my colleagues what they say to those objections?

- Have I found the answers or solutions to the objections on that list?

- Am I now confident that I can handle any objection?

Be proud of your price

Price-condition; 'What is the discount?'

Price is important, yet it is also unimportant. I have already said that people will find the money for the things that they really want. Fascinatingly, the more they want something the more the price importance becomes diminished.

In the B2B marketplace, professional buyers have to buy on behalf of their companies products and services that they don't personally need or want. Nevertheless it is their job to buy in order for their company to function. Many buyers believe that it is the duty of the professional buyer to buy the cheapest. This belief normally manifests itself in buyers who have had no training, as trained professional and skilled buyers realise that value is the major buying criterion.

It is essential to understand the buying process and what causes people to make a decision, who they buy from and at what price. Those influences we have already covered in some detail.

There is one massive misconception, and that is that customers want only to buy the cheapest. Therefore, if sales people have a product or service to sell that is similar to a competitor's, they will only be able to make the sale if they are the cheapest. This is known as the sales person's disease **'price-itis'**, and once caught it is very difficult to cure.

I have heard countless times from failed sales people bemoaning the fact that their products are too expensive. If they were a little cheaper then they could sell that much more. Now let's be realistic. If this were really true, why employ sales people? All you need is some good-quality price lists and to mail them out.

Statistical information has shown that approximately 20–25 per cent of people will buy only the cheapest product or service, regardless of whether it works. Approximately 1 per cent of people will buy only the most expensive. That means that the vast majority of purchases are transacted on some other basis. You know exactly what I am going to say – this is called 'value for money'.

In the current economic climate there is a natural trend within the buying public and in business to be more price sensitive. Nevertheless the major criterion will still be value for money. We all know that consumers can buy a motor car over the internet and save anything from £3,000 to £15,000. Some people will do just that. But has the motor trade as we know it ceased to function? No, because people would prefer to have the security of a motor dealer, a person to talk to and a local after-sales service.

Very few products that are the cheapest are the biggest sellers. Is the cheapest car the biggest seller? Is the cheapest supermarket the most successful? Are the cheapest clothing chains the most successful or profitable? We have all heard the expression 'You get what you pay for.'

The job of sales people is to sell when they are not the cheapest. The role of sales people is to sell at a profit, thereby helping their company to be profitable, to stay in business and to pay all the staff. As we know, it is the customer who pays the wages.

This chapter is titled 'Be proud of your price'. Professional sales people sell value not price. Don't ever be afraid of or embarrassed of your prices. Be proud and be positive, because any fear will be conveyed instantly to the customer. If you subconsciously think that you are too expensive or if you think that you might lose out because of your price, your manner, your body language and your lack of enthusiasm will betray you. If you are asked about your prices, be proud, don't make excuses and don't apologise; be prepared to give your prices even before you are asked. The more confidence and pride that you demonstrate in your prices, the more confidence your customers will have that they are purchasing value for money.

Have you noticed how some shops don't price their merchandise? I am sure your reaction is the same as mine: 'If it is not priced, it must be expensive.' The more people try to hide their price the more they convey the message that they are embarrassed about, not confident about and most certainly not proud of their price.

Price-condition

Please do not assume that price is not important. Virtually no sale ever takes place without the price being declared, discussed, negotiated or agreed. Most of us when we find a product or service that we want will enquire 'How much?'

Now there are some occasions when it is necessary to price-condition prospective customers or even find out what their perspective of the price may be. There are some occasions when your prospect will have no idea how much things cost. To save an embarrassing situation and also to prevent a price objection, it is very ethical and decent to price-condition.

What this basically means is that you make your customers aware without offence but at the same time that you find out exactly which product or service would best suit their budget. Here are some questions that will help towards price-conditioning.

'May I ask if you have a budget?'

'Do you have a sum of money in mind?'

'Roughly how much were you planning on spending?'

'To give you some indication, it could be between £300 and £800. Will that be OK?'

'I anticipate the overall cost to be approximately £80,000. Will that be all right?'

'I think it may end up at about £15,000. Is that about what you were expecting?'

'I can't be specific but it will be in the region of £6,000. Is this within your parameters?'

'What is the discount?'

Over the last three of four years there has been a tendency not only of the professional buyer but also of the consumer to get a discount. You may have already been asked 'So what's the discount?' This is now of course bordering on negotiation, which I am not going to go into in detail in this book. Suffice to say, a good sales person is not a price crumbler. Many sales people succumb to the temptation to reduce their prices as soon as they are put under a little pressure. Good, effective sales people defend their prices logically by reinstating the value.

If I am ever asked the discount question, my reply is always the same. 'Do you mind me asking why you want a discount?' The reply to that question is always not only great fun but fascinating. I have had these responses many times:

> **'Well, I always get a discount.'**

> **'My boss expects me to get a discount.'**

'I get a discount from...'

'It's my job to get a discount.'

'Well, I was hoping that you would give me a discount.'

They are the most common, but I am sure that you can add to them. What is really interesting here is that what is important in these examples is that the discount is more important than the actual end price. Here is a rather fun albeit facetious response, but be careful if you are going to use it:

'So the discount is really important to you.'

'Yes, Really important.'

'How much discount were you hoping for?'

'Well, 10 per cent.'

'Well, if I give you a different price and then give you 10 per cent off, will you then be happy?'

There are of course occasions when it is right and proper to give a discount, and that is when you negotiate different terms. For example, you can say to your customer:

> *'Now, if you have five of these I will give you X discount.'*
>
> *'If you pay up front I will give you X discount.'*

Always try to trade a discount with a change of terms or an increased order.

Key Questions

- Do people buy the cheapest?
- Do people buy the most expensive?
- Do people buy value for money?
- Do I price-condition?
- Am I a price crumbler?
- Do I make profitable sales and keep people employed?

(10)

Presenting a proposal

How to present a proposal

A comprehensive guide to proposals is beyond the scope of this book. I do, however, want to give you a few basic guidelines that will enhance your success rate when proposals, quotations or estimates are involved.

There are so many variables that, in order to give you some effective guidance, it will be necessary to be fairly general. It must also be accepted that there can be a big difference between a B2C estimate or quotation and that required for a B2B proposal, which normally entails a more complex solution to a business problem. Nevertheless, there is one point that sales people often fail to take into account. The first paragraph of the proposal or estimate must state the result of the product or service that the customer is buying, and that result should be the same as the result the customer is looking for. You can then include the price after you have stated the result.

Whenever you are asked to put forward a proposal or similar, before you leave the meeting you should run through various action points.

First, where it is agreed to put forward a proposal or similar, ask your prospective customer exactly what he or she wants. Ask and find out how much detail is wanted. Does the prospective customer want an outline as well as a more detailed document? This will not only save a great deal of wasted time on your part but will also give the customer a document or e-mail to read rather than skim through or be bored with.

Then, before you conclude your meeting, agree a day, date and time to return with your proposal – more on this later.

Written proposals really need to meet two most important criteria: first, they should have a good and logical structure; and, second, they should be written in good English, in other words in jargon-free, easy-to-read sentences. Please don't be verbose. A sales proposal will have a clear structure only if there is clarity of thought, which is why it is so important for you to find out exactly what your prospective customer wants to have included.

So what should be included in a proposal? This will be very general, but how about putting yourself in the other person's shoes? What do you require in that document to help you make the right and best decision? Did you find out before you left the meeting that your prospective customer might be showing the proposal to and discussing it with another person – maybe even a board of directors? It is important to be aware, if there are people you will not be speaking to who are going to be involved in the decision-making process, that your only chance of giving them the best selling information is in that proposal document.

The proposal therefore should be a stand-alone document that, when picked up and read, follows the classic sales presentation format and also the mnemonic AIDA. So right at the beginning there should be a section putting your neck on the line by stating and declaring the result of your product or service if the prospect should proceed and you should win the business. The customer is buying the result. The 'how to' will be explained in the proposal, in other words what you will be doing or supplying that will enable your company to give the customer the result that the customer is seeking. Let me again remind you: you are the solution specialist, and in this instance you do not start with the problem but give the solution first and then present the problem and the detail.

It is of course quite right and proper to supply and to present your suitability and your credibility. This can be at the end of the proposal. The majority of the proposal should be very logical. The logic must be convincing and justify the buyer's decision to proceed, even though that decision may have subconsciously been emotional.

Whenever you have had an estimate or quotation, what have you looked for first? No doubt you are exactly the same as me and have looked at the price. Some people try to hide the price (no doubt because they are embarrassed). Some people attempt to make it complicated. Therefore, make it easy for customers. If they are going to look for the price first without reading the document, I suggest that you put the price in at the beginning as well as at the end. If you follow what I am saying, you should put the price immediately after the section where you have put your neck on the line and stated the result of what your product or service will deliver to the customer.

How to present a proposal

At the meeting where a proposal or estimate has been agreed, there is as a way of moving to the next stage a straightforward process of putting yourself in control by delivering the proposal personally and creating an opportunity for a further meeting to close the business. Here is a sample conversation:

> *'Thank you, Ms Prospect. I should have the proposal completed within the next three days. Today is Monday. I can get it back to*

you by Friday. Which will be more convenient? Morning or afternoon? What time would be best?'

Agree the time

If you want to be a really successful winner of business, do exactly what I am stating here, and that is always to deliver a proposal personally and not put it in the post. When you take the proposal you are then in a position to go through it, check if the prospect is happy with it and then close the sale.

The also-rans in the business world work hard to get the chance of preparing a proposal document. They work really hard in preparing and putting it together. They then put it in an envelope with a creepy covering letter that finishes with 'If I can be of any further service, please do not hesitate to contact me.' These individuals have made the classic mistake of giving the next move to the customer. They have lost control.

So whenever possible always retain the next move yourself. Always take your estimates and proposals to the customer. Always tell your customers what is going to happen next.

With the ever-increasing pressure for speed and a fast response in business, e-mail or fax is of great use. There are some occasions when it is just not feasible, cost-effective or possible because of distance to take a proposal. This is where e-mail comes into its own. If you cannot visit send your document, but always sign off with the following:

> *'I will call you within the next few hours, first to make sure that you have received this e-mail and secondly to check that this is what you wanted.'*

You are now in a position to take control again, discuss your proposal and close the sale.

Key Questions

- Should I ask what the proposal should contain?

- Will I get more sales if I put the proposal in the post?

- Do I put the result first in the proposal?

- Is it a good idea to hide the price?

Great tips for sales success!

- Don't sit in reception areas as this reduces your confidence. Always remain standing.

- Don't say 'Thank you for your time.' It is really creepy, and you don't mean it anyhow.

- Try, in your mind, to understand the difference between a 'want' and a 'need'.

- Use stories, facts, statistics and examples – they are very helpful for your customers' ability to make up their minds.

- Go for a trial order: 'Try 10 of these on a test basis.'

- Get your prospects to talk to satisfied customers.

- Begin with a close: 'Would you like to own this car?'

- Cement a sale or order with a small deposit.

- For price-conscious buyers, don't defend your product and price. Sell the benefits and build the value.

- Understand the importance of the close. You either sell or you will be outsold.

- Always assume that the customer will buy.

- Go for a decision – a 'Yes' or a 'No' but not a 'Maybe'.

- When the prospect says 'Can I have…?', write it immediately on your order form.

- Ask 'Is it important when you take delivery of…?' If the prospect says 'Yes, I need it in 30 days', your sale could be complete here.

GREAT TIPS FOR SALES SUCCESS!

- Drawing a sale to a conclusion is automatic when you ask the right questions.

- Learn not to fear asking for the order. So what if they say 'No'? It is a 'No' before you've asked.

- Be a good-news carrier. Always have some good news for your prospect.

- Keep physically fit. More oxygen in the blood makes a more awake and alert sales person.

- Mentally debrief after each presentation – the good, the bad and the ugly. How could you have done it better?

- Outstanding service alone can become the greatest winner of business.

- Don't have pound signs in your eyes. You will never be a professional sales person while adding up your commission.

- Don't ignore other people – wives, husbands, secretaries, assistants or juniors.

- You are in the people business. So every meeting, every presentation and every conversation should be different.

- Your communication must reflect your personality.

- Good words and bad words:
  — Don't say 'change'; say 'improve' or 'develop'.
  — Don't say 'pay'; say 'own' or 'invest'.
  — Don't say 'sign'; say 'agree' or 'authorise'.
  — Don't say 'when I sell'; say 'when you own'.

- Do say 'Thank you' when you get an order.

12

Why Richard Denny Equals Sales Success!

The BBC claims that *"Richard is a legend on the international speaking circuit"*.

The Daily Telegraph describes Richard as *"The UK's guru of motivation"*

Whilst the Times says he is *"The master of professional salesmanship"*.

His motivational behaviour-changing sessions have also been called:

"Memorable" Daily Mirror

"Outstanding" NatWest

"Beyond Excellent" SDL International

"Inspirational" HSBC

"Exceptional" Mr Electric

"A great investment" Crown Timber

"In December 2007 I travelled from Bulgaria to have 1 hour of Richard Denny's time and that 1 hour earned me €300,000 in the following twelve months. That was 3 times what I had earned the previous year. I simply cannot recommend him highly enough."
Malcolm McDowell, Bulgarian Investments

"You helped me to create a series of large extremely profitable businesses".
Alan Jones OBE, Former ex Group MD of TNT Express

"Richard Denny's excellent practical tips will assist and motivate even the most reluctant".
Mike Crawford, Regional Service Manager, ABB Limited

"If every manager practiced the messages from Richard Denny their results would be awesome".
Philip Williamson, Former CEO Nationwide

"Before any person is given the responsibility of managing and leading others it should be a prerequisite to read Richard Denny's work".
Henry Pitman, Former CEO Tribal Group Plc

"Richard Denny provides great inspiration and his work 'Motivate to Win' is a must-have for all those who have to lead".
Brian Smart, Director General, British Franchise Association

"My first sales course with Richard Denny in Scotland fundamentally changed my life".
David Carroll, MD Stonor Search and Selection Ltd

"Richard Denny is an amazing straight-talking humorist and highly professional".
Professor Colin Turner, Psychology of Corporate Entrepreneurship

"I learnt from Richard about things I'd never heard of in business school".
Justin Miller, Explorer

"I am a sales manager in Portugal as a result of your teachings".
Aldérito Lopez

"Denny products are all about delivering excellence with consistency".
Michael Green, Partner at Hamilton Bradshaw Venture Partners

"Richard Denny's work has been instrumental in providing me with a framework to success".
John B Hackett, Chief Operating Officer, HSBC Bank

"Your work has been introduced to my sales force in Chile, because it works".
Ronald Verzijl, HIAB, Chile

"Thank you for a memorable inspirational event."
Advertising Director Ireland, Daily Mirror

"I confess to feeling nervous before the day started, but it quickly became clear you were going down well. A big thank you."
Partner, KPMG

"What a great success you made our convention. A smash hit."
Chief Executive, Molly Maid

"Richard did an outstanding job in engaging our Management Team."
H.R. Director, Sara Lee Courtaulds

"Thank you for an excellent contribution."
Regional Manager South West, Friends Provident

"Your speech was well received by everyone."
**Head of Donor Response Services,
National Blood Service**

"Thank you for a truly wonderful day."
Group Sales and Marketing Director, Lovells

"The feedback received showed unanimously that delegates found your presentation both inspirational and very informative."
**Marketing & Events Manager, Business Link,
London North West**

"The high quality of your presentation was much appreciated."
Director General, British International Freight Association

"Your presentation proved enlightening and valuable to our Client Relationship Managers."
Director Client Relationships, Coutts (Guernsey) Ltd

If you would like to find out more about courses and training run by the Richard Denny Group take a look at www.richarddenny.co.uk/

About the author

Richard Denny is one of the United Kingdom's leading authorities on winning business and selling. He has improved the skills of more than one million people worldwide with his teachings, books, certificated courses and sales diplomas.

Richard is chairman of the Richard Denny Group, which specialises in business training and executive recruitment. He is also non-executive chairman of three other companies.

Richard Denny is the most inspirational business speaker in the United Kingdom. He is probably unique in that his presentations not only motivate, inspire and educate his audiences, they also take away highly practical ideas that achieve enhanced performance. He is so confident that he guarantees to get an outstanding result. If not, his fee is refundable. You can't expect better than that (and it has never happened to date).

He has sold and marketed in the Middle East, where his products included steel, cement, Yugoslavian lamb and electronic equipment. With all this vast experience he was continually being asked to speak to and advise others, and this led to the Richard Denny Group being formed.

Over the past 20 years Richard has become a legend on the international speaking circuit. The Richard Denny Group is recognised as being at the forefront of business training on selling, leadership and management, customer care and business growth.

Richard has authored and presented over 40 training videos/CDs and 50 audio programmes. He is the author and presenter of three audio albums. His six books – Selling to Win, Succeed for Yourself, Motivational Management, Speak for Yourself, Communicate to Win, Winning New Business – are international best-sellers, selling into 46 countries and translated into 26 languages. Selling to Win has become required reading for anybody who wishes to aspire to becoming a sales professional, and this book is probably the world's best seller on this subject.

Richard is the creator and founder of the British Professional Sales Diploma and the British Leadership & Management Diploma. He is also chairman of a telecommunications company in the United Kingdom.

He is a broadcaster, writer, married to Dorothy with six sons, and is an enthusiastic player of numerous sports. His presentations are liberally illustrated with anecdotes, people stories and of course that delightful Denny humour. He talks common sense and has the knack of being a brilliant communicator. Apart from his experience as a keynote speaker, he also acts as a conference chairman and facilitator.

The Richard Denny Group
1 Cotswold Link
Moreton-in-Marsh
Gloucestershire GL56 0JU
Tel: +44 (0) 1608 812424
Fax: +44 (0) 1608 651638
Email: success@denny.co.uk
Website: www.denny.co.uk

Urbane Publications is dedicated to developing new author voices, and publishing fiction, non-fiction & verse that challenges, thrills and fascinates. From page-turning novels to innovative reference books, our goal is to publish what YOU want to read.

Find out more at
urbanepublications.com